Things TO DO in Young People's Worship

BOOK 2

SUSAN SAYERS

First published in 1999 by
KEVIN MAYHEW LTD
Buxhall
Stowmarket
Suffolk IP14 3DJ

© 1999 Kevin Mayhew Ltd

The right of Susan Sayers to be identified as the author
of this work has been asserted by her in accordance
with the Copyright, Designs and Patents Act 1988.

All rights reserved.
No part of this publication
may be reproduced, stored in a retrieval system,
or transmitted, in any form or by any means,
electronic, mechanical, photocopying, recording
or otherwise, without the prior written permission
of the publisher.

0 1 2 3 4 5 6 7 8 9

ISBN 1 84003 331 2
Catalogue No 1500251

Cover design by Jaquetta Sergeant
Edited by Peter Dainty
Typesetting by Louise Selfe
Printed in Great Britain

Foreword

While many churches provide for the needs of children, there is often an uncomfortable gap where young people are concerned. This is the age when deep questions are being asked, and it is essential that our young people find in their churches those who are going to listen and not be shocked; who are willing to enter into real discussion and provide relevant and unsuffocating support during adolescence.

Many churches are well aware of the needs, but find it difficult to provide for them. They are concerned about this age group feeling too old for children's ministry but not able to relate to what the adults are doing in church. Sadly, the result is often an exodus of young people, just when their faith could be (and often is) taking off.

Not only do our young people need the church; the church badly needs its young people. Their insistence on rejecting every hint of hypocrisy and their gift of presenting challenging ideas with wit and enthusiasm – these are good for everyone and vital for a healthy body of Christ.

This book aims to provide relevant and varied activities for young people, which stimulate their thinking and encourage valuable discussion. Although some young people will be involved in the children's ministry team, I am convinced that they need to be provided for at their own level as well. Sometimes I have suggested that the young people put their ideas to the wider church. Do encourage the church to take such ideas seriously.

A note about role-play

Improvising a drama is a very effective way of helping people get 'under the skin' of Bible and other stories. Precisely because of that, it is vitally important for the leader to 'de-role' the actors after it. This is simply and effectively done if the leader goes round the group asking each one to say his or her name, where they are and to define their real relationship with other actors, e.g:

What's your name?
 Joanna Harrison.

Where are you?
 Bethany Baptist Church youth group.

And do you *really* hate Karen?

No, that was just an act. We're friends.

This can be done in a very light-hearted way, adding to the fun of the role-play itself, and may seem quite trivial. However, for people of any age who have 'thought themselves into' a part, it's absolutely essential they 'talk themselves out of it'.

I hope the ideas in this book will enable young people in the churches to grow strong and healthy in their faith.

Recommended Bibles

It is often a good idea to look at a passage in several different versions before deciding which to use for a particular occasion, especially if you plan to involve several people in the reading.

For young people the New Century version of *The Youth Bible* includes various anecdotes and Bible studies which are inviting and challenging. A vivid version of the New Testament and parts of the Old Testament in contemporary language is Eugene Peterson's *The Message*. This catches the imagination and aids understanding. It is particularly good for reading aloud. *Into the Light* by the Bible Society is specially developed for reading aloud to those unused to the traditional language of the Church.

SUSAN SAYERS

Contents

THE NATURE OF GOD
    God's creative power   8
    God wants to save us   9
    The generosity of God   10
    The full picture of God   11
    The Lord provides   12
    Ready to receive God's gifts   14

JESUS CHRIST OUR LORD
    Jesus in danger   18
    Jesus grows up   20
    Jesus the Messiah   22
    Jesus and our expectations   24
    The resurrection and the life   26
    Jesus the Word   28
    The second Adam   30

DISCIPLESHIP
    The twelve disciples   34
    The demands of discipleship   36
    The way of suffering   38
    The power to endure   40
    The reward of faithfulness   42
    Resisting temptation   44

THE CHRISTIAN LIFE
    The way of true happiness   46
    Building on rock   48
    Priorities   50
    True riches   52
    Love as you love yourself   54
    Loving our enemies   56
    Forgiving one another   58
    Examples to inspire   60
    The wind of the Spirit   62
    Spirit of wind and fire   64

THE NEED FOR CHANGE
    God wants to make us better   66
    Facing the truth   68
    Repentance means change   70
    Kindly warnings   72
    Getting things straight   74

CHRISTIAN TEACHING
- The meaning of baptism — 76
- The meaning of marriage — 78
- The meaning of love — 80
- The full meaning of God's law — 82
- The Bible and prayer — 84
- Listening to God's word — 86
- Life after death — 88
- Seeing and believing — 90

INDEX OF USES — 91
- Topics
- People
- Activities
- Bible References

THE NATURE OF GOD

God's creative power

Thought for the day 'He commands even the winds and the water and they obey him.'

Things to read Genesis 2:4b-9, 15-25
Psalm 65:6-13
Luke 8:22-25

Things to do *Aim:* To look at God as worthy to receive glory, honour and power because he created all things.

Have a hands-on session, supplying magnets, iron filings, wire, batteries and light bulbs, so everyone can experiment with making circuits and seeing the magnetic patterns on paper.

Talk about the complexity of our universe, and have library books and science textbooks available with pictures of natural power, the planets and detailed organisms too small to see with the naked eye. Draw attention to the order, attention to detail, beauty and power of it all, and the way it all points to a caring, intelligent and generous Creator. The Bible's two creation stories in Genesis 1 and Genesis 2 direct us to see all this is brought into being by the wise and loving God. As you read the older story of creation in Genesis 2, keep track (on a sheet) of the things God does and says.

God's creative power wasn't only at work a long time ago 'in the beginning'; it is at work all the time. See Psalm 65 for examples of this.

Now read the story of Jesus calming the storm, listening out for evidence of God's power.

Discuss why Jesus agreed to calm the storm. What do they think might have happened if he had been allowed to go on sleeping? Talk about any times they have wanted to shake God into action when it feels as if he is asleep, and about what actually might be happening. Do we have Jesus 'in our boat' at home or school, or when we are with our friends? Do we 'wake him up'? Does his presence in the boat with us help us in any way?

Things to discuss 1. In what ways is God 'in charge' and in what sense is he not?

2. Do we cherish creation as the work of the God we know and love, or do we take it for granted?

God wants to save us

Thought for the day — Keep asking for God's Spirit and he will keep pouring out his blessing on you.

Things to read — Genesis 18:20-32
Psalm 85
Luke 11:1-13

Things to do — *Aim:* To know that God wants to save us and see us grow as Christians.

Tip out a pile of bits and pieces, and get everyone picking out the sweets from among the muddle.

Explain about Sodom and Gomorrah in the Genesis passage. Here is an example of things getting so bad that the whole society is heading for destruction. But someone is prepared to plead for these people. Using different voices read the conversation with God and Abraham. Abraham was loving like God loves – wanting to save people. We put some effort into simply untangling the sweets. Since we are so precious to God, he puts in huge effort to sort us out.

Now look at the passage from Luke, and the way Jesus teaches his disciples about prayer. Go through each phrase, making sure the meaning is clear, and then read the section on asking. Does Jesus mean we can ask and receive anything we want? Why does he sometimes say 'No' or 'Not yet'? Why does he want us to ask?

When we enrol on a course, we couldn't at that stage take and pass the final exam. But the hope is that if we go to all the classes and do the work we're given, we'll end up confident to take the exam and pass it. When we commit ourselves as Christians, that's also like a beginning, and we'll only develop and bear spiritual fruit if we take advantage of the teaching and feeding God provides for us. We need to ask God for it, and go on asking and receiving.

Things to discuss —
1. Do we assume God to be more tolerant of wrong than he really is, or doubt that he can really be as forgiving as he is?
2. How would you help someone to understand God's character when they've prayed for something faithfully and it hasn't materialised?

The generosity of God

Thought for the day — We have no right to be envious at the generosity and mercy God shows to others.

Things to read
Jonah 3:10-4:11
Psalm 103:1-13
Matthew 20:1-16

Things to do

Aim: To look at the nature of God's generosity.

In a circle pass round a twenty pound note (or a Monopoly equivalent). As it gets to each person they say how they would spend it if it was theirs, and next time round they say who or what they would give it to and why, if they were going to give it away.

Before you read the passage from Jonah, remind them of the rest of the Jonah story so they can see this part in context. Encourage them to bring out Jonah's anger in their reading. They can turn to Psalm 103, verse 8, to see where Jonah was quoting from as he grumbles at God. How does God treat Jonah? Does he argue with him, or shout back? No, he keeps Jonah safe while he calms down a bit and then teaches him a lesson. How? (Read verses 6-11.)

Now look at the parable Jesus told in Matthew 20. It can be read as a group, with parts being taken by different voices. Had the workers agreed a fair wage before they started? Why were they grumbling, then? Point out that it was the owner's right to be generous with his money – and the all-day shift were not losing out. Jesus wanted his hearers to see that whether people came to faith early or late in life, God was simply overjoyed that they were saved. We don't earn our right to everlasting life in any case; new life is a freely given gift, and we shouldn't ever begrudge people having it, even if we feel we have worked harder for God or our church than they have.

Things to disucuss

1. Are we happy to do God's work, or would we rather do our work, maintaining our control, and offer it to God complete?
2. Are we still expecting God to keep to our rules and guidelines? How can we avoid this in all our planning and church activities?

The full picture of God

Thought for the day — Jesus gives us the full picture of the nature of God.

Things to read — Exodus 33:18-23
2 Corinthians 4:1-6
John 1:14-18

Things to do — *Aim:* To see the picture of God shown in Jesus compared with the Old Testament view of God.

Mount a good poster-sized picture on card, and cut it into squares. Put dice numbers on the back of each piece and arrange the whole picture face down on the floor so that only the numbers show. The dice is thrown by everyone in turn, and a piece with that number on is turned over, so that the picture is gradually revealed.

Point out how we gradually understood more and more about the full picture as we saw more and more of it. It was the same with the people of Israel gradually getting to understand more and more about the nature of God. Read the Exodus passage, and talk about what it shows us about their understanding of God, as well as God's actual character.

When Jesus came to earth in person, it was like seeing the whole picture. Read the passage from John, and talk about what Jesus tells us about the nature of God which people couldn't see clearly before. How does John contrast Jesus with Moses?

Then read Paul's words in 2 Corinthians. Do people today still have incomplete pictures of God, in spite of what Jesus has shown us? What about superstition, belief in fate, or the idea that disease and accidents are sent as a punishment? What other distorted views of God can they think of?

Things to discuss

1. How do these readings trace a developing understanding of God's nature?

2. What difference should Jesus's view of God make to the way we live our lives?

The Lord provides

Thought for the day — Jesus shows us in action the loving provision of the God who made us.

Things to read
1 Kings 17:8-16
2 Corinthians 9:6-12
John 2:1-11

Things to do

Aim: To look at God's provision for us in the light of the Old and New Testament readings.

'I need . . .' The leader needs various items which either individuals or teams can supply, depending on your numbers. Here are some suggestions:
- a 'pear' (they could bring a pair of shoes)
- fourteen pounds (a stone)
- a long hand (a watch)
- a piece of keratin (a hair)
- a hole (a sock or sweater, indicating the ankle or neck hole)

Point out how they were all able to supply your needs, often in rather unusual or surprising ways. Our God knows what our needs are, and his nature is to provide for us. Show the following symbols as you talk about each point.
- *A globe.* Sometimes he does this through the huge bounty of creation, which we are asked to share and look after responsibly.
- *Wrapped presents.* Sometimes he will provide for us by giving us the courage, gifts or energy we need to carry out the work he asks us to do.
- *Wire bent into a question mark.* Sometimes he will answer our prayers differently from the way we would expect. For instance, we may pray for an end to a job we loathe, and God may provide us with a more positive attitude to where we are, so that eventually, looking back, we can see that his way was best.

Now read the passage from 1 Kings 17:8-16, with different people taking different parts. Talk about the way

God provided for the widow and her son, and for Elijah. Keep a note of the ideas raised.

Next read the account in John 2 of the wedding at Cana. Add to the ideas about how God provides for the host and the guests, and for us, reading the passage. Does God turn water into wine at any other time? Help them to understand that this happens over a period of months every year. We so often take for granted the everyday ways that God provides for us, and this is a good opportunity to celebrate them.

Things to discuss

1. Do we sometimes hold back from asking for God's help in case it turns out that he isn't able to/doesn't want to do anything about our problem? (N.B. God *always* answers us when we pray, though it may well be in a different way from what we expect.)

2. How willing are we to take on the obedience that Mary recommended? ('Do everything he tells you.') What holds us back?

Ready to receive God's gifts

Thought for the day — When we recognise our dependence on God we will approach him with true humility and accept his gifts with joy.

Things to read

Isaiah 58:9b-12
Psalm 104:10-24
Luke 18:9-14

Things to do

Aim: To look at God's gifts poured out on us when we are right with him.

A 'correct alignment' challenge. Place a marble on a chair, and a tray on the floor about one metre away. Provide an assortment of tubes. The challenge is to get the marble from the chair to the tray, using the tubes. This will only work if they get the tubes lined up correctly.

Point out how the marble wouldn't have arrived at the tray unless they had got the tubes right. God pours out the blessings of his Spirit on us, but if we are not right with him we can't access them in the same way. Read the passage from Isaiah 58, bearing in mind that Isaiah is calling the people to realign their lives to God's values.

We need to be aware of all God gives us. Read Psalm 104:10-24 and make a group list of God's amazing provision in our own lives which we so often take for granted. Talk, too, about the temptation to live as independently of God as possible, believing that we as humans are in control, and forgetting that there would be no such thing as life if God hadn't thought and loved it into being.

Read the Luke passage, where Jesus is drawing attention to wrong attitudes to God and one another in our praying. Have different people reading the different parts, and discuss the reason why Jesus said that the tax collector went home right with God rather than the Pharisee, even though the tax collector was obviously not a paragon of virtue. What does this say to us about our prayer life? Record some guidelines for a good and valuable prayer life which you can pick up from the story. (Examples might be being honest with God, telling him how we really feel, recognising his power in our lives, valuing his love and help, asking him for insight to see what needs changing and help in doing something about it.)

Along the pieces of tube write: 'Line yourself up with God's values and receive his blessing!' Then line them up again and send lots of marbles sliding down the tubes and into the tray.

Things to discuss

1. What kind of things in life remind us of our need of God, and what kind of things give us a false sense of superiority and independence of him?

2. What is your hope in God based on?

JESUS CHRIST OUR LORD

Jesus in danger

Thought for the day Jesus lived in the real world of physical danger.

Things to read Exodus 3:7-10
Hebrews 2:10-18
Matthew 2:13-23

Things to do *Aim:* To understand the risk God was prepared to take in coming to save us.

Rescue! Play this game in which someone needs rescuing from a magic castle. (This is a chair with a length of rope on the floor encircling it.) The only way to break the evil magic is to get the key which fits the lock. (This is a rectangle of card from which a key shape has been cut. The key has been cut into several pieces. When the group has collected all the pieces the completed key should fit the card shape.) Hide the pieces around the building, and pass a dice round the group. When anyone throws a six they can go hunting for a piece of the key.

Read Exodus 3:7-10. We can see that God loves his people and really wants to look after them and save them. But, what are the risks involved if God comes in person to save the world? Make a note of their ideas.

Now read the Gospel, looking out for the risks and dangers. Make a note of these too. Through Joseph and Mary working with God, the baby is kept safe, at least for the moment. What happened when he grew up? Was the risk worth taking if Jesus was going to end up being put to death? Again, make a note of their ideas.

Finally read Hebrews 2:14-18 to see what this writer feels about the risks involved in God coming to live among his creation. (The risk was worth taking because it meant that through becoming human and sharing human experiences, Jesus could really help us and save us, even though it meant that he had to suffer death in the process.)

Things to discuss

1. From the reading of today's Gospel, what kind of person does Joseph seem to be, and what can we learn from him that might help us in dealing with crises in our own lives?

2. What was the advantage of Jesus being born as a human baby, rather than appearing as an adult to save the world?

Jesus grows up

Thought for the day — Jesus' perception and understanding of his purpose and work begins to take shape throughout his childhood.

Things to read

1 Samuel 3:1-10
Philippians 2:5-8
Luke 2:41-52

Things to do

Aim: To explore what it meant for God to be taking on the clothing of humanity.

Have an assortment of dressing-up items and give each small group a character. Using the items available, they have to dress one member of the group appropriately and the other group(s) try to guess who or what the dressed-up person is supposed to be. Possible ideas: Father Christmas, Minnie Mouse, a Power Ranger, a bride, a mountaineer.

Read together the Gospel story, with different people taking the parts. Focus on what was going on in Jesus' mind while he stayed behind in the temple, asking questions and listening to the teachers. What questions might have been coming into his mind about himself?

They can make a note of the suggested questions. (They may well include things like: Who am I really? What am I supposed to be doing in my life? How am I going to explain this to everyone? Can these writings be talking about me? How could these people have written about me when they don't even know me yet?)

Compare Jesus's experience of growing self-awareness with the experience of the boy Samuel (1 Samuel 3:1-10), and with your own experience of growing up. Are there any similarities?

Refer to the way we dressed up to become someone else. The word 'Incarnation' (write it down) means being clothed, or embodied in flesh – in other words, God taking on humanity. Round the word, write some of the things that you all think of about what that meant and how it might have felt, bearing in mind Jesus at twelve years old in the temple. The sort of ideas you come up with might include: risky, dangerous, confusing, humbling, scary, exciting, heartbreaking, puzzling, nerve-racking, thrilling.

Finally read the Philippians passage which draws together the areas you have been exploring and sums them up. These are words worth learning by heart, or practising saying together over a background of music in church.

Things to discuss

1. How does the story of Jesus in the Temple add to our understanding of what the Incarnation means?

2. God gives us our own special clothing as Christians – see what it is in Colossians 3:12-14. Are we wearing it?

Jesus the Messiah

Thought for the day — Jesus is recognised and pointed out by John to be God's chosen one.

Things to read — Isaiah 49:1-7
John 1:29-42

Things to do

Aim: To explore why the disciples thought Jesus was the Messiah.

Giant Mastermind. Fix up three chairs as shown below, with three pieces of coloured card hung round the back, so only the person behind the chairs can see the colours. In front of the chairs have a length of lining paper marked out as shown. People use crayons or marker pens to record their guess as to the colour and position of the hidden colours. The person behind the chairs responds by placing a tick for every correct colour and for every correct position. Eventually they should be able to work out the exact hidden pattern using reasoning and deduction.

Draw their attention to the way we had to work out the answer to that puzzle by going on the information we were given, linked with a 'hunch' that our idea was right, and a little help from our friends. That's what the first disciples had to do.

As they read John's Gospel, they can look out for the puzzle they were trying to solve (Who's this?), and notice how they did it. Record their observations. What information did the disciples already have about the Messiah? Read the passage from Isaiah, and again record their observations. (One day God's anointed One – the Messiah – would come in person to save them and set them free. It wouldn't be just for the people of Israel but for the whole world.) Who gave them other hints and clues? (John the Baptist; their brothers and friends; Jesus' conversation.) Unlike the Gospels of Matthew, Mark and Luke, John has the disciples recognising Jesus as the Messiah almost as soon as they meet him. He may well be emphasising the way Jesus' glory shows, to us as well as them, when we enter into a relationship with him.

Things to discuss

1. What can we learn about evangelising from today's Gospel?

2. How does John's way of narrating Jesus' Baptism differ from Matthew's? What do both accounts agree about?

Jesus and our expectations

Thought for the day   As Jesus rides into Jerusalem on a donkey, and the crowds welcome him, we sense both their false expectations and his own sense that suffering and death are near.

Things to read   Isaiah 50:4-10
Luke 19:28-40

Things to do   *Aim:* To look at the statement Jesus made by his entry into Jerusalem and the mixed reactions to it.

Tales of the unexpected. Sit in a circle. Each person in turn adds one word to make a group story. Draw attention to the way the story ends up quite different from what you expect from the word you added, because different people have different ideas and plans.

Have a large sheet of paper with a picture of the entry into Jerusalem in the middle. Round the outside of the picture work together on comments and questions which different people might have made at the time. What might the children have thought and wondered? What about Peter, Judas, Mary, Lazarus, the Pharisees, and the Romans? Put their suggestions in speech bubbles, identifying the speakers.

Now read the Luke version of Jesus' entry into Jerusalem with different people reading the parts, and everyone being the crowd.

Make a short radio documentary with an interviewer asking various representatives what they think against the crowd background and a commentator describing what is happening. You could use the following script as a framework. * = sound effects of the crowd.

Commentator: * Good morning. I bring you live to the stretch of road approaching Jerusalem. Here in the Kidron valley the way is filled with crowds * and it looks as if the person they're all waiting for is coming. I must say he doesn't look very grand. He's riding a donkey! But the crowds seem excited enough *. Excuse me, Sir, who is this? *(Man replies)* And you, Madam, why are you here today? *(Woman answers)* People have torn off branches * from the palm trees to wave, and as Jesus comes nearer they are actually throwing their coats down on the ground. They obviously think him very important indeed. Excuse me, you are one of his close friends, I believe. What do you think this is all about? *(Peter replies)* The children are joining in too. Just listen to them! * Well, the procession has moved on through the city gates now. One thing is certain, this man Jesus has the hearts of the people: they're greeting him like a king! *

Things to discuss

1. Was there any way the suffering and death of Jesus could have been avoided?

2. Do we have any false expectations of Jesus?

The resurrection and the life

Thought for the day

Jesus is the resurrection and the life. He can transform death and despair, in any form, into life and hope.

Things to read

Ezekiel 37:1-14
Romans 6:1-11
John 11:1-45

Things to do

Aim: To explore the ways in which Jesus is the resurrection and the life.

Use a paper kit for constructing a skeleton, or make a simplified home-grown one from thin card, following the illustration below.

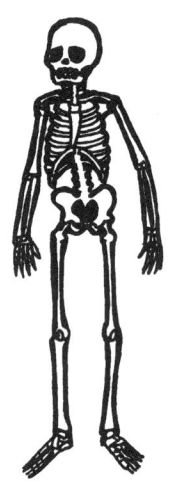

First explain that the people of Israel were living in exile, and felt there was no hope for them when Ezekiel had this vision. Then read the Old Testament passage, with some of the group providing sound effects with percussion instruments or blocks of wood, or even gently moving a pencil up and down between their teeth. What would this image have said to the people, bearing in mind where they were coming from? Bring out the message of hope and God's capacity for transforming even the deadest situation.

What about the dead situations in our world and in our own life? Write some of these down on paper and then read the story of Lazarus. Several people can take part in this reading, or it could be acted out. What has it to say about some of the situations you wrote down? What does it tell us about Jesus and who he is?

Read Romans 6:1-11 and see how Paul links the idea of death and resurrection to Christian baptism.

Things to discuss

1. How would the image of dry bones help the exiled people Ezekiel was called to speak to?

2. Compare the responses of Martha and Mary and Thomas. What do we learn about the strengths and weaknesses of each?

Jesus the Word

Thought for the day — The grace and truth revealed in Jesus show God's freely-given love.

Things to read

Genesis 1:1-3
Hebrews 1:1-3
John 1:1-18

Things to do

Aim: To explore the nature of Jesus as the eternal Word.

One person in the group is given a chart to follow like the one below. This person gives the instructions out so that eventually everyone is arranged on chairs in the way shown on the chart.

Discuss the impressive effect of the spoken instructions. Words spoken can bring creative things about. An orchestra or band can play out the ideas in the composer's mind. A book (show some examples) can take you off to other countries or other ages in your mind, just through the words on the pages. Words have power.

Now read John 1:1-18, checking for meaning as you go along. Link the first three verses with the first few verses of Genesis and help them see the connections. (Pick up on the darkness in which the loving Word brings light; how is that true of both passages?) Draw their thinking together in the last verse: the Son has shown us what God is like. Explain that the Greek word for 'word' (logos) meant any kind of communication, much as we might 'say it with flowers' or describe someone's actions as 'speaking volumes'.

Things to discuss

1. What has or would it cost you to receive Jesus into your daily living, your work, leisure, politics, finances and popularity?

2. Is it worth it?

The second Adam

Thought for the day — Jesus knows all about temptation; and he can deal with our sin.

Things to read
Genesis 2:15-17; 3:1-7
Romans 5:12-19
Matthew 4:1-11

Things to do

Aim: To explore the way Jesus is seen as the second Adam.

Reversals. In pairs, work out a simple sequence of actions both the right way round and in reverse – for example, walking to post a letter; opening a present and being pleased with it; hammering a nail and hitting your thumb; packing a suitcase. These can be written on cards and given out to the pairs who work on them and perform them to the group in the reverse way first, seeing if people can guess from the reversal what the real action is before it is acted out.

Today we are going to look at the greatest reversal of all time. Begin with the Genesis reading, encouraging different people to take the speaking parts, but as always being sensitive to readers who lack confidence or fluency. Try to get at the real sin of disobedience to God, and explain that Adam and Eve are the archetypal human beings, blowing it as they succumb to temptation in their weakness. We fail. We mess things up. We cannot put things right by ourselves.

Now read Romans 5, verses 17 and 19. This whole passage is so dense that I suggest you only look at these two verses which focus on the link between Adam and Jesus and the reversal of humanity's disobedience through Jesus' total and loving obedience. Talk about how Jesus showed that obedience, both in his life and his death, and how he did for us what we could never do for ourselves, purely out of love for us.

Finally look at Matthew's account of Jesus' temptations, to see his obedience in action right at the beginning of his ministry.

Things to discuss

1. Can we help one another more to resist temptation or is this always a battle we have to fight on our own?

2. How are Adam and Jesus similar, and how are they different?

DISCIPLESHIP

The twelve disciples

Thought for the day

Jesus sends his ambassadors out to proclaim God's kingdom and bring hope and peace of mind to the harassed and lost in every age.

Things to read

Exodus 19:2-8a
Romans 3:21-26
Matthew 9:35-10:10

Things to do

Aim: To look at the sending-out of the twelve and its relevance for contemporary mission.

String up a length of washing line with pegs on it. Have a chart with everyone's name on, and let each person have a go at collecting the pegs one-handed. The aim is to hold as many pegs as possible in that one hand. This score can be entered against the names. The prize for the winner? A peg.

First read the passage from Exodus, with all of them reading what the people said. From what they know already, did the people keep their word? No, they didn't. Talk about the problem that humans have of being unable to pull ourselves up by our own bootlaces. We can't save ourselves, but now Jesus has done for us what we could never do ourselves. Read Romans 3:21-26 to see how Paul explains this.

Go over with them the fact that Jesus needed to train a small team of people to carry on the work of spreading this good news, so that everyone in the world can benefit from it, and live their lives in a state of inner peace instead of turmoil and being harassed all the time. How many disciples (students) did he choose? Twelve. Do we know their names? Collect as many as they know and supply the rest. Today we are going to read about the time when Jesus sent these twelve out on mission.

Read Matthew 9:35-10:10 with a list headed 'Kit list', which has these items on it: extra pair of boots, spare coat, lunch bag, money, staff. When you come to verses 9-10, cross off each item as it is mentioned. Why might Jesus have sent them out like this? Talk together about how they were to go first to the 'lost sheep of Israel' (link this with the Exodus reading), and how, having few possessions and living simply like this, they could act out the message of trusting in God and being happy whether you have loads of comforts or not. Point out that these particular instructions were sensible for that time and landscape, but the principle of living simply – so that you are available to 'travel light' wherever God calls you, and have more time for people – still holds true today. The Church is still called to go out, without lots of wealth or power, and preach the good news and bring God's wholeness to people.

Does the church do this well, partly, or hardly at all?

Things to discuss

1. Is it foolish to talk about rejoicing and suffering in the same breath?

2. How would you interpret Jesus' instructions to the twelve for workers in the harvest today?

The demands of the discipleship

Thought for the day Following Jesus is expensive – it costs everything, but it's worth it.

Things to read Proverbs 3:1-12
Hebrews 12:3-11
Luke 14:25-33

Things to do *Aim:* To explore the implications of the high level of commitment Jesus speaks about.

Skills which require lots of concentration. Give out a balloon each, and work at keeping it in the air, using only knees and feet. Try juggling, either with the proper balls or with rolled socks or bean bags.

Those skills demanded a lot of concentration. Today we are looking at what Jesus told his followers about the level of commitment needed to live God's way.

First read the Luke passage, using either the New Century version (both the *International Children's Bible* and the *Youth Bible* have this) or *The Message*. The translation is important because this passage can be easily misinterpreted and these versions are quite helpful. Draw attention to the sensible, practical way Jesus has of ensuring that we all know what we are taking on. He doesn't want us to have any illusions. We need to know that following him means being prepared to 'let go' of plans, possessions and people, so we have a different attitude to life, and travel light.

That doesn't mean that Jesus wants us all to rush off and leave our families and friends. Our God is a God of love, and those kinds of demands are not in his agenda at all. But changed priorities are part of our decision to follow Jesus. We are placing God at the very centre of our life, and that will affect our very closest relationships and our dearest ambitions. Even these dearest things and people need to be valued in the context of our love for God, and must not become alternatives or substitutes for God.

Look at the passages from Proverbs and Hebrews. Note how seriously they take the need for full commitment. Note also the link between the word 'disciple' and the word 'discipline'.

Our walk with God is a two-way relationship. As we come to each choice, each problem and each stage of life, God will help us and work in us so that we keep on the right path – the path which is marked out by the 'Love God and love one another' signs. That path may well take us through some exciting and dangerous terrain, and it will not always be comfortable; it's more like back-packing than a holiday cruise. It's a great adventure, and one we need to take seriously, and prepare for, so we're not caught unawares by the first storm or rock-face.

Things to discuss

1. Why is discipline so important in life? Is it any less important in the Christian life?

2. How would you justify the costliness of following Jesus?

The way of suffering

Thought for the day

As Jesus prepares for the necessary suffering of the cross, he is tempted, through well-meaning friendship, to avoid it.

Things to read

Jeremiah 15:15-21
Hebrews 2:10-18
Matthew 16:21-25

Things to do

Aim: To look at why Jesus had to suffer and why Peter's advice was rejected.

Give out road maps and ask them to find a motorway route to Manchester from London which will avoid Birmingham in the rush hour. (They will find this is virtually impossible without a vast detour!)

Today we are looking at how some things have to be faced and can't be avoided, however much we would like to side-step them. First tell them about a prophet called Jeremiah, who never found it easy to be God's spokesman but knew that was his calling. Today's reading finds him full of doubts and fears, pouring his heart out to God. Read up to verse 18. Do they ever feel like this? Is it OK to talk to God like this? Yes, it is! God wants us to come to him 'real', wherever we happen to be. Part of prayer is working through our feelings of anger and resentment, with God who can help us with them.

Now read God's reply to Jeremiah, verses 19-21. See how God shows Jeremiah where he is wrong, but also promises his total support through the suffering Jeremiah is bound to have in this calling. If we offer ourselves for God to use, he will use us, and that might involve us in conflict or suffering. God doesn't enjoy that happening, but he needs people who are willing to suffer, so that the work of setting people free can go on. And we are never expected to work on our own, but always yoked up with him, and that eases the load.

Now look at the Gospel, where Jesus, in his human nature, is dreading and fearing the suffering of the cross, while at the same time, in his divine nature, he can see it as the glorious plan of salvation which will bring hope to the world. He can't afford to be tempted to side-step the suffering which is all part of the package.

Then read the passage from the Hebrews which throws more light on why Jesus had to suffer.

Things to discuss

1. How can we ensure that our well-meaning friendship never becomes a stumbling block to another's spiritual growth?

2. Are we prepared to accept the cross God needs to lay on us, or are we trying to remain in control and choose our own?

The power to endure

Thought for the day When things get difficult God gives us power to see it through.

Things to read Joshua 1:1-9
2 Timothy 1:1-14
Luke 12:35-43

Things to do *Aim:* To explore the way God gives us the strength to endure to the end.

Ping. You will need some empty Smartie tubes, complete with lids. This may necessitate bringing full Smartie tubes and eating the contents! Mark a line on the floor to stand behind and measure how far everyone can ping the lid, by holding the tube and thumping it with their fist. (This is a game my daughter and her student friends devised one evening, from an upstairs room in their hall of residence.)

First read the passage from Luke's Gospel and notice how important faithfulness and patient endurance are in those who follow Jesus. But where can we get the strength to keep going when things get tough?

Work out the physics behind the 'ping' game. The lid is propelled forward by the sudden rush of air behind it. It wouldn't be able to move any distance at all on its own.

We need the power of God's Spirit to urge us forward and move us into action; it is God who provides us with the strength and courage to suffer for the Gospel. Without that power and encouragement we could easily become downhearted and discouraged. Read Paul's letter to Timothy, where Paul has found that God's power makes him quite happy to accept the dangers and difficulties that go with the job of working for the spreading of the kingdom.

Then read Joshua 1:1-9 and note how Joshua was encouraged to lead the people into the promised land, knowing that God was with him.

Look at some examples of Christians who have persevered in difficult times or jobs, such as Desmond Tutu and many others under Apartheid, Floyd McClung in the red light district of Amsterdam, and people in your own parish.

Things to discuss

1. Has the message of the media – that it is normal and our right to be happy, wealthy and healthy – given us false assumptions and expectations in this age?

2. What benefits does God manage to harvest from suffering, provided we allow him to work his redeeming love in the situation?

The reward of faithfulness

Thought for the day — At eight days old, Jesus is presented in the temple, and at the Purification is revealed to Simeon and Anna as the promised Saviour who is able to reveal to us our true selves.

Things to read — Habakkuk 2:1-4
Psalm 37:3-9
Luke 2:22-40

Things to do —

Aim: To see how Simeon and Anna's faithfulness and trust were rewarded, and relate this to our own faith.

Play a trust game, such as making a close circle around one person who starts to fall in any direction. The circle of people around them prevents them from getting anywhere near the ground. Today we are looking at two people who knew they could really trust God.

Read the Gospel passage together, with different people taking the parts of Simeon and Anna. Discuss *who* was involved, *what* happened, *where* it happened, *when* and *why*. Draw out the fact that both Simeon and Anna had been faithful in prayer for many years, so that they were able to recognise what God was saying to them, and trust him to do what he said. They had also learnt to be obedient. (Suppose Simeon had decided not to act on God's nudging to go to the temple that day.)

On a sheet of paper, write in the middle: 'What about us?' Around this question jot down what Simeon and Anna can teach us about good practice in our own lives. (This may include such things as the value of regular daily prayer, getting to know what the Bible says, listening to God as well as talking to him, doing what God asks straight away, trusting God, being patient, being prepared for God to answer our prayers in unexpected ways.)

Use the sheet you have completed and go round the ideas, asking God to help us grow in each of these areas.

Give each person one of the ideas to express in mime and present this with a reader as part of the service.

Alternatively, write and illustrate each point and make a display for the church or for the magazine headed 'Learning from Simeon and Anna'.

Things to discuss

1. What enabled Simeon to recognise in this baby the promised Messiah?

2. What can we do to stay spiritually supple all our lives? What might make us spiritually stiff in the joints?

Resisting temptation

Thought for the day — Following his baptism, Jesus is severely tempted out in the desert, and shows us how to overcome temptation.

Things to read — Deuteronomy 8:1-6
1 Corinthians 10:12-13
Luke 4:1-13

Things to do

Aim: To explore the way Jesus stood up to the temptations and overcame them.

No 'yes' and 'no'. One person is asked all sorts of questions by the group and must reply to them without saying 'yes' or 'no'. If they do, someone else has a go.

In the game we were all trying to make the volunteer do the wrong thing. It is very hard to resist temptation, especially in areas where we naturally find ourselves wanting to do the wrong thing. Today we are going to look at how Jesus managed to resist temptations that were very strong.

Read the story of Jesus' temptations in Luke and then, using three sheets of paper, look at each temptation in turn, under these headings:

1. What did Satan say?

2. What was wrong about his suggestion?

3. How did Jesus reply?

4. Where did his quotation come from?

When you have looked at all three temptations, show a fourth sheet with the heading 'What about us?' Work out together a few hints picked up from Jesus to put into action whenever we are tempted. Some of these may involve getting prepared in advance (such as knowing the Bible well enough to use it).

Things to discuss

1. Jesus must have wanted his disciples to know what had gone on in the desert or he wouldn't have told them about it. Why do you think he thought it was important for them to know?

2. Share any tips you have found helpful in overcoming temptation.

The Christian Life

The way of true happiness

Thought for the day   The challenges and rewards of living by faith.

Things to read   Jeremiah 17:5-10
Psalm 1
Luke 6:17-26

Things to do   Aim: To be introduced to the beatitudes and explore their meaning.

Write the following items on separate pieces of card (have several sets if the group is larger) and have everyone discussing how to place them in order of importance in life.

> Happiness
>
> Having my own way
>
> A job with power
>
> Lots of money
>
> Pleasing God
>
> Good friends
>
> Helping other people
>
> Having children

First set the Gospel reading in its context as Luke has arranged it, immediately after the choosing of the apostles and the growing hostility towards Jesus from the religious authorities. Ask some of the group to imagine they have just been chosen and have agreed to be apostles, with a dangerous and insecure future ahead of them. Ask others to imagine they have thought of following Jesus but decided it's too risky and they'd rather keep their money, security and friends. Now read the Gospel together, with a narrator and a different voice for Jesus.

Have a brainstorm of how the 'apostles' feel, listening to what Jesus has been saying, and how the others feel.

Now read the passage from Jeremiah and see how it links up with what Jesus was teaching. What about us? Where do we stand?

Things to discuss

1. How is our own society cursed, or damaged, by widespread trust in what people say, make and sell?

2. Are the beatitudes impractical and idealistic, or simply too challenging to accept?

Building on rock

Thought for the day

Wise listeners build their lives up on the strong rock of the word of God.

Things to read

Deuteronomy 11:18-21, 26-28
Romans 7:18-8:4
Matthew 7:21-29

Things to do

Aim: To explore what it means to build our lives on the rock of God's teaching.

Beforehand make a simple picture of a house, cut from coloured paper. At the same time cut enough identical pieces for each couple of people in the group to make up the same picture. (You might have background pieces of green and blue, a different green hill, the main house shape, different coloured window and door shapes.) The pieces will need to be put together in the right order and position if they are to look exactly like the original.

First show the original to everyone for twenty or thirty seconds, and then cover it up while they all make their own pictures. Then show the original again to check who got it exactly right.

They probably noticed in that activity that they had to concentrate carefully during the viewing time so as to pick up and store as much vital information as possible. Then, building on that, they were able to get close to the right picture. Today we are looking at something Jesus said to some of those who came to listen to him. They claimed to be his followers but in fact their lives showed no attempt to carry out God's teaching.

Read Matthew 7:21-29. If we really listen to what Jesus tells us – listen with our heart and will as well as our ears – we shall be wanting to use what we have heard in the building of our lives. If, on the other hand, we assume those words are not really meant for us, and have no intention of acting on them, we shall be throwing away all that Jesus offers, and end up building our lives on things that give way on us and let us down, instead of the solid rock which we can always rely on.

In the Old Testament the people had tried all kinds of ways to remind themselves of God's Law so that they would remember how to live his way. Read the Deuteronomy 11 passage to see how seriously they tried.

To some extent it worked, but then the reminders themselves would start to become more important to people than what they were there for! With the coming of Jesus, and the filling of our lives with the Holy Spirit of God, there was a drastic and exciting change to this state of affairs. Paul talks about it in today's passage from Romans: we know we can't manage it on our own, but through God's freely given grace, won for us by Jesus, the impossible becomes possible.

Not only can we listen to Jesus' words, and make the decision to build on that strong foundation, but God will also be there with us in the work of building.

Things to discuss

1. What does it mean to 'do the will of my Father', rather than saying only, 'Lord, Lord!'?

2. What could be a practical present-day equivalent of the Deuteronomy advice for reminders that we are God's people?

Priorities

Thought for the day

When we are willing to take up our cross with Jesus we will also know his risen life.

Things to read

Daniel 6:6-13, 16-23
Romans 6:1b-11
Matthew 10:24-39

Things to do

Aim: To look at what it means to put God first in our lives.

Prepare fourteen sheets of paper as shown below, and arrange them in the right grid but the wrong order. They have to rearrange the letters by sliding the sheets, one move at a time, like those interlocking tile puzzles. If it gets too frustrating they can cheat and simply arrange them by the number guide so that they end up with the correct message.

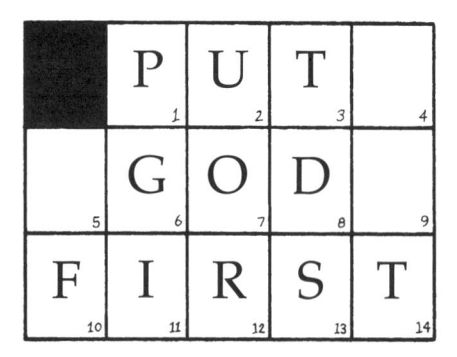

	P	U	T	
	1	2	3	4
	G	O	D	
5	6	7	8	9
F	I	R	S	T
10	11	12	13	14

Talk about how difficult it can be to get things in the right order of importance in our lives, and how getting the wrong order in life can be a messy business (like opening your bottle of ketchup before shaking it). More seriously, wars can cause a vast number of people to suffer, all because greed or power is a top priority rather than co-operation and sharing.

Read Matthew 10:24-39, to discover what Jesus has to say about what is important, and which things we should take most seriously. Notice how for God all our details – even the number of hairs on our head! – are very important because to him we are so precious. That's why he was willing to go through anything for us, even a tortured death. If Jesus is worth following at all, he is worth following closely, and to do that we really do need to put him first in our lives.

Look at the passage from Romans 6 to see how following Jesus into resurrection life will make us dead to some things and alive to others. Some things will no longer have their hold of importance (like what?), and others will become more and more important to us (like what?).

Things to discuss

1. If we think of ourselves as dead to sin and alive to God, how will we react in times of temptation, and when we are despised or ridiculed for our faith?

2. Obviously God wants us to love the people in our families, so how can we expect them to take second place to God in our lives, especially if they themselves are not believers? (Clue: think of a hosepipe fixed on to the water supply, compared to a water butt. How many buckets could get filled in each case?)

True riches

Thought for the day

True richness is not material wealth; true security is not a financial matter.

Things to read

Ecclesiastes 2:1-11
1 Timothy 6:6-19
Luke 12:13-21

Things to do

Aim: To explore what is real wealth.

On a long roll of wallpaper, stick a line of objects from magazines and catalogues. Split people into pairs and one of each pair looks at the line of objects as it is pulled past them (as on a game show). Then they have to tell their partner all the things they can remember, with the partner writing them down. Both get a sweet or a penny for each object remembered.

Read Luke 12:13-21, putting in sound effects and having different voices. Notice what had happened just before Jesus told the rich fool story, and that will help them get at what the parable is about. Compare the rich fool with the writer of Ecclesiastes 2:1-11. Make a list of ideas about the different things people use to protect themselves and make them feel safe and secure. Help them to see the limited value of some things and the good, lasting value of others. Read 1 Timothy 6:6-19 and find those things which give us true riches.

Act out the following short sketch and prepare to perform it in church if appropriate.

A   I've got a new bike with 36 gears.
B   Well, I need a new bike with 36 gears. I'll ask my parents.
C   Why shouldn't I steal a bike? I'll never have the money to buy one.
A   I'm going to Florida again this year.
B   We could go to Florida if I persuaded Mum to work more hours.
C   It's not fair. Everybody else goes to Florida. We stay with Nan at Clacton.

A	I am a rich fool.
B	I am an envious fool.
C	I am a resentful fool.
A, B, C,	And we're all trapped by money!

Things to discuss

1. Is it possible to live in our culture without becoming materialistic?

2. How can we help people see the value of this longer-lasting spiritual wealth? And do we still need convincing ourselves?

Love as you love yourself

Thought for the day — We are to love God with our whole being, and love others as much as we love ourselves.

Things to read

Leviticus 19:15-18
Psalm 1
Matthew 22:34-40

Things to do

Aim: To see how the whole law and teaching of the prophets are summarised in Jesus' words.

Put a few crisps or mini-doughnuts on pieces of kitchen paper, and everyone can try eating them with their hands behind their backs. It makes you realise how clever we are at training our arms and hands to provide lovingly for our every need.

Every day we get our arms to feed and dress us, switch on the television and the toaster, and open doors. That is a caring consideration, or love, that comes as second nature to us. We are told in the Bible that we are to love God, and love our neighbour as we love ourselves.

Start by reading Matthew 22:34-40 (just the summary of the law section). Notice how Jesus says that on these two commandments hang all the law and the teaching of the prophets. Show them a parcel with this summary on the label. If you unpack this (do so), you are looking at the whole word of God. (There's a Bible inside.)

Did Jesus make this summary, or was he quoting from somewhere in the Old Testament? He was actually quoting from the book of detailed instructions on ritual and practice for the Levite tribe of priests. In our Bibles it's called the book of Leviticus. Read the passage from Leviticus, with its rules for every eventuality, but also the sound advice to love others as much as we love ourselves.

Why does loving others as we love ourselves incorporate all those other laws? It's because if we showed to others the kind of attentive caring we lavish on ourselves, there would be no lying, stealing, murder, adultery, envy or lack of respect. All those things happen because we are not thinking considerately of the other person or people.

How does the first commandment fit in? As we love God, establishing him as number one in our lives, his love pours out to us, enabling us to love others in this attentive, considerate way.

If you have time, read Psalm 1, where the trees beside the water flourish and fruit, just as our lives will if we live by those two basic commandments.

Things to discuss

1. What advantage is there in a general summary of the law over the detailed rules system?

2. How does this summary of the law affect the way we live?

Loving our enemies

Thought for the day

We are called to be as perfect in our generous loving as God our Father is.

Things to read

Exodus 23:4, 5, 9
Romans 12:14-21
Matthew 5:38-48

Things to do

Aim: To explore the implications of loving our enemies.

Friend or foe? Have a number of qualities written on cards which can be sorted into the 'friend' or 'foe' pile. Ideas for the cards:
- Lets you down all the time
- Lends you their kit when you have forgotten yours
- Mistreats someone you love
- Accuses you so you get the blame unjustly
- Puts you down in front of other people
- You can trust them to keep a secret
- Makes you pay for everything and never offers to help
- Cheers you up when you're feeling down
- Winds you up constantly
- Waits for you if you're late out
- Keeps your place in the queue
- Understands when you don't agree about something

Read together Matthew 5:38-48. Begin by clearing up a common misunderstanding about Christians and enemies. There are always some people we get on really well with, and others we dislike. It is natural to feel hostile to anyone who treats you or your loved ones badly. God knows about all this. He knows we have both friends and enemies, and he doesn't want us to pretend about our true feelings.

We are not told to *like* our enemies, but to treat them with love. That means being absolutely fair and honest with them, however dishonest they are with us. It means treating them with respect and consideration, however much they insult and scorn us. That way we will be showing them the kind of behaviour we consider right, and we won't have been dragged down to their level.

What Jesus doesn't mean is for us to lie down like doormats for people to walk over! If an enemy is bullying us, for instance, the loving way to treat them is not to suffer it all in an agony of silence and fear, but to tell them that they are behaving badly, and let someone in authority know, so that the situation can be properly dealt with.

We also need to look at our own behaviour. Are we sometimes behaving as enemies to people in our own families, for instance? Are there people we despise, or treat badly, or refuse to help?

Being holy means behaving in a godly way to everyone, without drawing a line round a particular group we give ourselves permission to hate.

Things to discuss

1. Is Jesus' teaching unworkable? Or is it simply more challenging than we would like to take on seriously?

2. How does our society's concern with self-value and self-assertion fit in with our Christian faith, and where does it clash?

Forgiving one another

Thought for the day — Jesus teaches us to forgive those who sin against us.

Things to read

Genesis 45:3-11, 15
Ephesians 4:1-3, 31-32
Luke 6:27-38

Things to do

Aim: To look at the practical implications of loving and forgiving one another.

In groups of two or three, have an argument using only strings of numbers to speak with. This takes away the embarrassment of having to think of actual words, but all the emotions can be heard loud and clear.

Ask them to imagine that they are meeting some people who beat them up and left them for dead a few years ago. What would they want to say to them now?

Read the passage from Genesis and see how Joseph's reaction compares with their own feelings. Talk over how Joseph was able to forgive his brothers as he did. Point out that God can always transform ugly situations so that some good comes from them, especially if we invite him into our hurt to work there.

Try acting out the following sketch.

LOVE ONE ANOTHER

Mum is putting the cleaner away. Dad is reading the sport page. Katrina is making her face up in front of the mirror. Michael walks in . . .

Mum — Hey, watch where you put your muddy feet – I've just cleaned that floor.

Michael — That's right – shout at me as soon as I put my face round the door.

Dad — Don't you talk to your mother like that, young man. I won't have it.

(Michael sees Katrina in his sweater)

Michael — Who said she could wear my sweater?

Katrina — *(Sighs)* I only borrowed it. *(She takes it off)* Here, catch. Have it back. It smells.

Michael — Cheek! It's better than the stinky perfume you're wearing. Skunk, is it?

Mum	Oh shut up, everyone. I can't stand living like this. Let's start again.

(They all walk backwards to their starting place.)

How do you think it would go if everyone was living by Jesus' teaching in Luke 6:27-38?

Now read the passage from Luke's Gospel. How does it match with Joseph's handling of his brothers, and with all the teaching today on self-assertion and self-esteem? What is the difference between loving your enemies and being a doormat and letting people walk all over you?

You could also read them an extract from the writing of Corrie Ten Boom who has much to say about forgiveness.

Things to discuss

1. What stops us from putting down our grievances? What might Jesus say about this?

2. Does our present concern with the importance of self-assertion clash with Jesus' teaching on loving our enemies?

Examples to inspire

Thought for the day In Christ we are chosen to be God's holy people.

Things to read Psalm 15
Ephesians 1:1-6 and 1 Peter 2:9
Matthew 5:1-12

Things to do *Aim:* To look at some saints as examples to inspire and challenge us.

What's in a saint? Give out the following criteria for saintliness, written out on separate cards, to each small group. The task is to decide the order of priority for being a saint. Give out edible rewards when the groups have completed the task.

- went to church a lot
- gave everything away
- lived a long time ago
- miracles happened when they prayed to God
- faced death rather than give up their faith
- showed God's love in their life
- were willing to do what God asked them to
- prayed a lot
- helped people a lot

Discuss the lists everyone has drawn up, and remind them that today we are going to think about those people who have lived out their lives as close friends of God, doing his will and following the rule of love. Then read the Beatitudes, pausing after each 'happy are' to question how these people can be called happy. Then read Jesus' reason for their joy.

What are we to make of this teaching? What sense does it make, and who among Jesus' followers would be likely to think it totally foolish?

Now show everyone an old family photo album. Point out that it is full of friends and relatives who are part of the whole extended family. There are some in the family to encourage the others by their example. In the Church, our stained glass and statues are a bit like the Church family album, and we find challenge and encouragement from the examples of courage and generosity we see in the saints.

Read Ephesians and 1 Peter, and notice the way it isn't just individuals who are to be filled with all the fullness of God's loving Spirit, but the entire Church of God. How is the Church doing at the moment, do they think? And how could it improve in this?

Design a stained glass window for a saint, emphasising the way that their example can help us.

Things to discuss

1. Would you be willing to suffer persecution for your faith?

2. Reading the passages for today, how does the Church of your experience live up to its calling?

The wind of the Spirit

Thought for the day — Anyone who receives the Spirit of God can be made new.

Things to read

Ezekiel 37:1-14
Acts 2:1-4
John 3:1-12

Things to do

Aim: To explore the meaning of Jesus' conversation with Nicodemus and its implications for us.

On separate pieces of card, write out the different descriptive levels on the Beaufort scale of wind force. In pairs arrange these in the right order to match the correct numbers. Have an electric fan blowing while they work.

Talk about the force of the wind and its invisible nature. You can hear it, and you can feel it's there, but you don't know where it comes from or where it's going. That's a bit like us understanding God's ways and moving where he takes us; though we have never seen him we can feel that he is there and we trust him.

Then read the account in John's Gospel of the conversation between Jesus and Nicodemus, with people reading the different parts. Why did Nicodemus find what Jesus said so hard to understand? To explore this, have a chart like this:

To understand God's ways do you need to be . . .
- well-educated
- important
- adult
- a religious professional
- thinking you know the answers
- set in your ways

or . . .
- open to teaching
- humble
- childlike
- seeking to know God better

- knowing there is lots you don't know
- spiritually flexible

Highlight the things Jesus was helping Nicodemus to understand about God's kingdom. In what ways was Nicodemus like this and in what ways did he need to change? Help them to recognise that to go with God does take a step of trust, which we all find difficult, and, the more in control of life we think we are, the harder it is to stop relying on all that and trust God instead.

Things to discuss

1. Would it seem more comfortable if we were able to earn our salvation by doing good things? Is it harder to accept God's love as a gift?

2. How would you answer someone who said you don't need to be born again if you were brought up to go to church.

Spirit of wind and fire

Thought for the day — As Jesus promised, the Holy Spirit is poured out on the apostles and the Church is born.

Things to read
Acts 2:1-21
John 14:8-17, 25-27

Things to do

Aim: To look at the continuing coming of the Holy Spirit.

Have two large sheets of paper, one with the word 'Fire' in the centre and the other 'Wind'. In small groups work on drawing and writing all the things they can think of associated with these words. Share the sheets with everyone.

Recap on the way the disciples were waiting for the Spirit promised by Jesus, and they were expecting something to happen, though they didn't know what it would be. Then read the passage from Acts together, involving everyone for the crowd, and for the sound effects. Ask them to close their eyes. Take them travelling through time, imagining that they are in the room with the disciples. Draw on the use of senses – what they can hear, smell and see, how their clothes feel and the heat in the room, and how it feels to be among these people who have walked about with Jesus and are all really praying.

Lead them to imagine the sound of that strong wind approaching, and then the experience of being surrounded with this powerful presence of God and the wind and flames of fire. Bring them back into the present and talk about the experience.

Then read John 14 and note that the Spirit is sent to guide us, empower us, teach us and fill us with God's peace.

Things to discuss

1. Do we really want God's Spirit to fill us, or does the thought terrify us so that we are actually asking God to keep a safe distance?

2. Why do you think Jesus said that even greater things would be possible for his Spirit-filled followers than had been done during his own ministry?

The Need for Change

God wants to make us better

Thought for the day   In Christ we become a new creation bit by bit.

Things to read
2 Kings 5:1-14
James 1:16-27
John 21:15-19

Things to do

Aim: To explore the way in which we are helped to grow spiritually by God's patient love.

Have packs of playing cards available, and in pairs build houses of cards. Admire one another's results before they collapse.

With the card houses we have been doing some delicate and painstaking building work. Explain how God works carefully and painstakingly with us in making us a new creation. It takes patience, gentleness and a very steady hand!

Read together the story of Naaman in 2 Kings 5. How much did Naaman want to be cured? Look at all the lengths he went to, and what it would be like for a person like him to have such a disease. What was it that put him off doing as Elisha recommended, then? How did he react after the seventh wash? Explain how Naaman was interested mainly in his skin being cured. God was also interested in his whole character and wanted to develop that as well.

Now read the passage from James. We find it easy to deceive ourselves. But if we say we want to be made new, when really we're only going through the motions and are not prepared to put what we've been taught into practice, that's not true religion. What God is interested in is people genuinely wanting to be made new. When that happens he's there like a shot, helping us to change things we'd never have thought we could, and setting us free from bad habits and wrong attitudes of a lifetime.

Finally read about Jesus' interview with Peter in John 21. After Peter's failure and denial on Good Friday, Jesus patiently restores and forgives him and prepares him for future service. So God is careful to rebuild our lives when we fail if we are willing to let him.

Give everyone a lump of clay. Put on some music (something from Delirious?, perhaps) and, as you mould the lump into a new creation, think of God moulding you and other people you care for into the new and fulfilling life God has in mind.

Things to discuss

1. What put Naaman off obeying Elisha's instructions? Are we sometimes put off obeying God's instructions and suggestions for similar reasons?

2. In what ways are we difficult for God to mould – like clay?

Facing the truth

Thought for the day — God sets his leaders apart to challenge people to face the truth.

Things to read

Jeremiah 1:4-10; 7:1-7
Hebrews 10:19-31
Luke 13:10-17

Things to do

Aim: To look at the way God calls people to challenge prejudices and assumptions.

Challenge. Deal out cards to everyone in each small group. Each player places a card face down on the table in front of them and says what it is. The cards should be placed in sequence, from ace to king, but players can pretend if they don't have the right card. However, if another player challenges them they must show the card they have put down. If it is wrong, they have to take their pile up again; if it is right, the challenger has to take the cards.

In the game, they were challenging those they thought were not telling the truth. Today we are going to look at how God challenges our lifestyles or attitudes or assumptions, when they are drifting away from the Law of love.

God always knows when there is a problem, because he sees into our hearts and minds. Since he is full of love for us, he doesn't look at any drifting away or wrong thinking and want to condemn us. He sees it and longs to put us right again. That means getting us to listen, which isn't all that easy, when we often walk through life with cotton wool in our ears, spiritually speaking.

Now read the passages from Jeremiah, drawing out God's method of calling a person from within or near the situation he wants to change, and giving them a charge, or commission, to speak out God's words. Their words will then carry God's authority, and enable people to look at how their living needs to be altered and improved.

Look now at how Jesus, the Messiah, did the same thing in action, when he healed the crippled woman on the Sabbath. Read the passage, noting the effect the healing had on those who had developed a distorted view of the Law. Sadly, they saw it not as a loving release in keeping with God's Law, but as rule-breaking, and therefore against God's Law. Jesus had to remind them of the importance of living by the spirit of the Law.

Finally look at the letter to the Hebrews, and discuss the challenge there to accept God's offer and live out our worship on a daily basis, not taking God too casually, nor despising the sacrifice of Christ.

Write down the names of those who have helped you to find out about God and grow closer to him, and put all these names on a sheet. Place candles among the names and thank God for these people and the way God has used them. Pray for each of them.

Things to discuss

1. Why were the religious leaders finding it so hard to accept Jesus when they already proclaimed their faith in his Father?

2. Why do many people prefer to steer clear of too deep an involvement with God in their lives?

Repentance means change

Thought for the day — John the Baptist appears with his urgent message of repentance, to prepare the way for the coming of the Messiah.

Things to read — Malachi 3:1-4
Luke 3:1-6

Things to do

Aim: To explore the nature of repentance and forgiveness as necessary preparation for welcoming Jesus into our lives.

Sketch to be read by different members of the group.

Patient 1 Doctor, doctor, I am sure I am a pair of curtains.

Doctor Well, pull yourself together! Next patient, please.

Patient 2 Doctor, doctor, I can't get to sleep at night.

Doctor Well, lie on the edge of the bed and you'll soon drop off. Next patient, please.

Patient 3 Doctor, doctor, everyone ignores me as if I'm not there.

Doctor Next patient, please.

Patient 4 Doctor, doctor, I demand to change my doctor!

Doctor Oh really? Why?

Patient 4 Your jokes are making me ill!

When people find their bodies are not working properly they usually go to a doctor (hopefully one with better jokes!) because they want their bodies sorted out. Often the way to recovery means doing something differently – having more rest, giving up smoking, taking medicine or more exercise, perhaps.

When John told the people that they needed to sort their lives out, it made them look at the way they were behaving. They could see that they were not actually living in the best way. They asked John to help them put things right, and John told them to repent so they could be forgiven.

To repent means to change direction and turn round. That is sometimes quite easy (deciding to give up swearing), and sometimes very difficult (forgiving someone who has hurt you a lot). But it is only when we recognise what is wrong in our lives, and really want to change direction, that we can know the relief and freeing that comes from God's forgiveness.

God knows that, and offers us all we need to be able to put things right. If we go to a doctor and the doctor offers us help, we'd be foolish not to accept. Yet often people will worry secretly about a sin they know they have a problem with, and not take up God's offer to help. People can change. You can change. And repenting and being forgiven opens life up again and feels very, very good.

Things to discuss

1. Luke wants to place John firmly in the historical context. How does he do this, and why?

2. 'Repentance for the forgiveness of sins.' Why was John told to preach this particular message at this particular time?

Kindly warnings

Thought for the day — It is our responsibility to encourage and uphold one another in living by the standard of real love.

Things to read — Ezekiel 33:7-11
Romans 12:3-18
Matthew 18:15-20

Things to do

Aim: To explore our responsibility as Christians to encourage and uphold one another.

Play 'pick-up-sticks', using either the bought game, or drinking straws or sticks. Having tipped all the sticks on to a table, each person has to try and remove one without any of the others moving.

What made it hard to move one stick on its own was that all the sticks were holding one another up. As Christians, we need to be holding one another up like that, in an interconnected heap of God's love and care, so that we can't easily be tempted away from living in God's promise.

Read the passage from Ezekiel 33. There are two important things to look at here:

1. If we don't warn people and encourage them to turn back to God when they are in the wrong place, we will be held responsible to God for them.

2. The last thing God wants is for people to perish, and he will always forgive; no one is ever a hopeless case.

It's a bit like those sticks again – if evil is trying to pull someone away, we need to start moving, supporting them so they are safe.

Now read Matthew 18:15-20, with Jesus picking up on the teaching in Ezekiel and giving us guidelines for dealing with situations where people need to be approached about how they are behaving, or about wrong attitudes. Have the process drawn out like a programme sequence (see below) and trace it through together.

The Need for Change

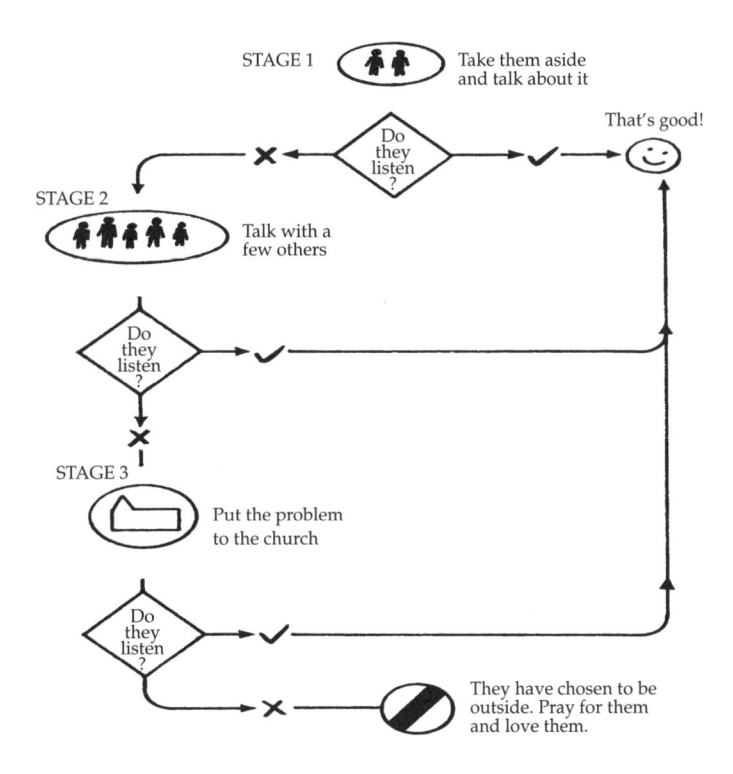

```
STAGE 1  [👥]  Take them aside
              and talk about it
         ◇ Do they listen?
           ✓ → That's good! 😊
           ✗ →
STAGE 2  [👥👥] Talk with a few others
         ◇ Do they listen?
           ✓ →
           ✗ ↓
STAGE 3  [📖]  Put the problem to the church
         ◇ Do they listen?
           ✓ →
           ✗ → ⊘ They have chosen to be outside.
                 Pray for them and love them.
```

Then look at the passage from Romans, to remind ourselves of what we are aiming at, and what those right attitudes are.

Things to discuss

1. Why do we instinctively draw back from facing someone with their sin and talking through it with them? Should we have a special ministry for this, or is it everyone's concern?

2. Where does welcome and acceptance of the sinner turn into a lack of concern for their behaviour which is damaging for them and the community?

The Need for Change

Getting things straight

Thought for the day — Straighten your lives out and live by God's standards of love.

Things to read — Amos 7:7-17
Deuteronomy 30:15-20
Luke 10:25-37

Things to do — *Aim:* To look at the message of Amos and the challenge of living God's way.

Choices. One person goes outside and the others decide which is the 'right' chair to sit on. When the person comes in they have to choose the chair they think is right. If it's the wrong one they get tipped off. If it's the right one they get a sweet.

First check that they know what a plumb line is and what it is used for. Then look at a map to see where Amos lived and how the kingdom was divided into Israel in the north and Judah in the south. Now read the passage from Amos, discussing how they might feel if they were being told by someone from the other nation that their behaviour needed straightening out, and how Amos would feel, as God's messenger.

In the starter activity we were having to choose 'blind', so there was no way we could be sure we'd chosen right. But God doesn't leave us to choose blindly; he has made the choices very clear (see Deuteronomy 30). If we live to please ourselves and indulge all our wants and fancies, we will be choosing destruction and death, and history has proved that true. If we live to please God, in a way marked by love for God and neighbour, we will be choosing fulfilment and life – both for us as individuals and for our society.

Now read the passage from Luke 10, and see how this story Jesus tells allows the expert in the Law to see more clearly so that he can choose which direction he wants his life to go. We are not told what decision he made.

Things to discuss
1. Why does human nature so often react to God's light as something to be deflected or shut out?

2. What should we do if we find God pointing out an error or sin in our life?

Christian Teaching

The meaning of baptism

Thought for the day

When Jesus was baptised, God confirmed his identity and his calling.

Things to read

Isaiah 43:1-2
Acts 8:14-17
Luke 3:15-17, 21-22

Things to do

Aim: To look at what Baptism means to us and what it meant to Jesus.

Give each small group a sheet of paper with the word 'Water' in the middle. Everyone writes or draws all the things that water does. Then the different sheets can be shared with the other groups.

Begin by reading the passage from Isaiah 43, noticing the personal calling by name, and the promise from God that we will be kept ultimately safe.

As you read Luke's account of Jesus' Baptism together, ask them to point out what the people were expecting of the Christ or Messiah, and what sign was given from heaven when Jesus was baptised. Do the two match up, or is there a contrast in the pictures used? Draw out the positive, and the gentle nature of the dove and the voice, compared with the thorough and quite aggressive 'cleansing' picture of the harvester sorting the wheat and burning the chaff. Also notice that the dove is a symbol of purity, and both pictures therefore describe a cleansing and saving.

Look at the sheets of paper with the 'Water' words on, and see how the idea of being dipped under the water in Baptism links up with these ideas of washing, drowning and sustaining new life.

Finally read the passage from Acts, and notice how the apostles were concerned that the new Samaritan Christians should have full Baptism, including the outpouring of God's Holy Spirit. How does this pattern link up with the practice in your own church? Discuss any questions they have, and have available some literature suitable for your own tradition for them to take and read if they wish.

Things to discuss

1. Obviously Jesus was not being baptised because he needed to repent of his sins and turn his life round. So why did he do it?

2. What is the significance of water in Baptism, and why did Peter and John place their hands on the Samaritan Christians?

The meaning of marriage

Thought for the day The love and faithfulness of husband and wife should reflect the love and faithfulness of God for his people.

Things to read Isaiah 62:1-5
Ephesians 5:21-33
John 2:1-11

Things to do *Aim:* To look at how God's glory is revealed in marriage.

Characters: Prospective bride and bridegroom, and the vicar.

Bride	This must be the vicarage. Sure you want to go on with this?
Bridegroom	Yeah, why not? The pub isn't open yet.
Bride	P'raps he'll offer you a drink? *(Rings doorbell)*
Vicar	Ah, good evening! Tracy and Martin, isn't it? Do come in.
Both	Thanks/OK. *(They sit on chairs)*
Vicar	I'm sure you'd like a drink . . .
Bridegroom	*(Eagerly)* Oh yes, please!
Vicar	Tea for both of you is it . . . with sugar?
Bridegroom	*(Disappointed)* Oh . . . er . . . yes, that will be great.
Bride	*(Whispers loudly)* Martin, behave yourself!
Vicar	Does he always do what you tell him?
Bride	Heavens, no. If I tell him anything he's more likely to go and do the opposite!
Vicar	What about that, Martin? Does she do what you tell her?
Bridegroom	Heck, no. She's really stubborn. It drives me mad!
Vicar	Mmm, I see. And you two are thinking of getting married, are you?
Bride	Yes, that's right. I've seen a fantastic dress and it's all covered in . . .
Vicar	How about you, Martin – how do you feel about getting married?

Bridegroom	Well, I don't mind either way, really, but it's a good excuse for a party, and she says her dad will be paying.
Vicar	Mmm, I see. Do you think you two could cope with a lifetime together?
Bridegroom	A lifetime? Cor, that's pretty steep, isn't it?
Bride	A lifetime? Is that what it means?
Bridegroom	Come on, Tracy, let's get out of here. Lifetime, indeed! Anyone would think I loved her! *(They exit)*
Vicar	*(Shrugs shoulders and shakes head)*

Why did Tracy and Martin not want to commit themselves to getting married?

Read the Isaiah passage together, to see something of God's nature, and then read the Gospel, with different people taking parts. What qualities of God expressed in the Isaiah reading can we see revealed in John's account of Jesus at the wedding?

God has given us the ability to love one another, and his complete love and faithfulness are reflected in the good, lasting marriages and friendships we see around us.

Things to discuss

1. Discuss Paul's view of marriage in Ephesians 5:21-33.

2. Is love more important than commitment in a marriage relationship?

The meaning of love

Thought for the day

Christ has shown us the meaning of love in his teaching, ministry and sacrifice.

Things to read

Leviticus 19:9-18
1 John 4:7-12
John 13:31-35

Things to do

Aim: To explore the nature of God's loving friendship with us and its implications for us in our relationships.

Bring along a selection of newspapers and cut out any stories and headlines which they feel are about a breakdown of love between individuals, groups and countries. Share the findings with one another.

Draw attention to the fact that they have collected plenty of evidence to suggest that people find loving quite difficult. Look at John 13 and 1 John 4 to see if these passages can throw any light on this for us. Presumably, if Jesus' followers are going to be noticeable by their loving, it's likely that most people will not be behaving in this way, and that ties in with what we have seen in the newspaper. The fact that the unloving behaviour is news, however, suggests that there are still lots of people who are living lovingly; they don't make the news because this is still considered normal behaviour, and that has a lot to do with our Christian heritage, and the spark of God's love in our human nature.

Have a brainstorm of the kind of behaviour Jesus might have had in mind when he talked about us loving one another, and collect the ideas on paper. Did he mean romance, hero worship, loyalty, co-operation, forgiveness, sex, caring for animals or the environment?

Look at how godly loving breaks down barriers between people and is never destructive or possessive, and then look at how this links with the words of Jesus that God would be glorified through the Crucifixion. Help them to see that Jesus' total love was shown on the cross in the way he was prepared to go on loving unselfishly whatever the cost.

Things to discuss

1. What does Leviticus 19:9-18 tell us about love in practice?

2. What areas in our church and in society would be transformed if we learned to love one another?

The full meaning of God's law

Thought for the day — To live God's way is to choose the way of life.

Things to read — Deuteronomy 5:1-22
Romans 13:8-10
Matthew 5:17-48

Things to do

Aim: To see how Jesus fulfils the Law.

Getting the whole picture. Cut up a large poster or picture into nine squares, and number the backs of the pieces. Arrange them upside down, but in the right order. Work out a quiz based on the ideas below but adapted to suit your group. Each time a question is answered correctly a piece of the picture is turned over, until eventually the whole picture is revealed.

Ideas for quiz questions:

Who won the last cup final?
Who scored?
Who were they playing?
What was the score?
Who was in goal?
What colours did . . . play in?
Who is . . . .'s manager?
What was the score at half-time?
Where was the match played?

or:

What's their latest release?
What are their names?
How old are they?
Name two of their hits.
What are the lyrics of . . . . ?
Who sings?
Who plays . . . . ?
What does . . . . like to eat?
Where do they come from?

Gradually, as we had more information, we got the whole picture. It was rather like that for the Jewish people, because they had gradually understood more and more about who God was and what he was like. When Jesus came and lived among them, he built on all that knowledge and experience, and showed them the whole picture by his life, death and resurrection.

Read the Matthew passage first, followed by the reading from Deuteronomy to see where the people were coming from, and compare Jesus' teaching with the commandments he refers to. How was it the same and how did it take the law and fill it with more complete meaning?

Things to discuss

1. How do rules help, and in what sense are guidelines sometimes more useful?

2. Why is it that when we have chosen to face life we still want to behave as if we are facing the other way?

The Bible and prayer

Thought for the day   Don't get side-tracked; always pray and don't give up.

Things to read
Jeremiah 31:31-34
Psalm 119:97-106
2 Timothy 3:14-4:5
Luke 18:1-8

Things to do
Aim: To learn the importance of Bible-reading and prayer in growing as Christians.

Around the room have some Bible references displayed, and in other places the appropriate verses written out, without references. Number the references and letter-name the verses. Everyone is given paper, pen and Bible, so they can discover which verses and references go together. Recap on how to look references up in the Bible if necessary. Choose for the references some they are very familiar with and some from recent weeks' teaching.

Check the Bible reference answers and point out how they are now able to find their way around their Bibles well enough to do that activity, which is excellent. Paul would be proud of them!

Read today's excerpt from Paul's letter to Timothy, so they can see that they are all following Paul's advice in learning from the Scriptures and getting to know them well. List the reasons given for Bible-reading being beneficial.

Read Psalm 119:97-106 to realise how important the reading of the Law (the Scriptures) has always been to devout Jews. Can it be any less important to us?

Now read the passage from Jeremiah, especially verses 33 and 34. Talk about how this became possible with the sending of the Holy Spirit when the Church was born – and we are part of the same Church here in this town today. God's Spirit enables us to grow as Christians, with daily prayer and Bible-reading to help us.

Show a school timetable, and talk about why we organise our day with Maths and PE nearly always at the same time every week. Bring out the value of regular structure and routine in developing skills. It's just the same with prayer. We need to be persistent in our prayer. Jesus told the story in Luke 18 to make this point.

Have a selection of daily Bible-reading schemes available to look at and discuss, together with various different Bible translations they may find helpful.

Things to discuss

1. Do we have God's word in our minds and written on our hearts? What can we put in place to improve our present situation?

2. If God knows our needs before we ask, why does Jesus advise us to be persistent in prayer?

Listening to God's word

Thought for the day — The meaning of the scriptures is revealed to the people.

Things to read
Nehemiah 8:1-3, 5-12
Psalm 19:7-11
Luke 4:16-30

Things to do

Aim: To see how God's revelation of himself to us is linked with our readiness to listen.

Play a brief game of dodge ball, using a soft sponge ball if inside.

Talk about what methods we use to switch off from something we don't want to hear (like pretending to be asleep, pretending not to have heard, or that we heard something else). God doesn't want to keep himself a secret, and is always showing us things that can help us get to know him better, but sometimes it's a bit like trying to get the ball through to the person in the middle – they keep turning away, and putting up barriers to stop themselves getting the message.

Read Luke 4:16-30 together, which includes the crowd's reaction to Jesus' teaching. Have different people taking various parts but ensure that the person who reads the part of Jesus is a sensitive reader; you may prefer to read this yourself, having prepared it well. Everyone can join in the crowd's words. Before you read it, ask them to be listening out for the barriers people were putting up against the truth.

After the reading talk over why the people first of all thought Jesus was wonderful and then turned against him. Draw out such things as: the difference between pride in a local hero, and faith in God; the craving for signs and wonders instead of goodness and truth; possessiveness – wanting to own and control Jesus; familiarity breeds contempt.

On a sheet of paper keep a record of the main ideas raised in the discussion. Show them a coin. If they think of this reaction as tails, we're now going to look at the heads reaction.

Turn to the Nehemiah reading and listen out for the contrasts. Both crowds are being shown new truths about God and his ways. How does this crowd react?

Record their ideas on the other side of the paper. Draw out such things as: when you come ready to listen you can hear; when the truth gets through to you it makes you want to change your life.

Things to discuss

1. Why do you think the people were encouraged to go and spend the rest of the day celebrating? Where does true penitence turn into a wallowing in guilt?

2. What kind of atmosphere do you detect in the event described in the reading from Luke? What might have blocked the people from 'hearing' what Jesus was saying?

Life after death

Thought for the day — Life after death is not wishful thinking but a definite reality.

Things to read

Job 19:23-27a
2 Thessalonians 2:1-5, 13-17
Luke 20:27-38

Things to do

Aim: To explore the evidence for believing in life after death.

Beforehand collect a tape of fragments of pop music. Play this and see if they can work out which songs the snippets have come from. (Or do this with TV programmes – either the dialogue or music.)

Like the little snippets of sound we've just heard, we are given little experiences of what heaven is like while we are still living on earth. Since life in heaven is life with God, we don't have to wait till we die to begin living our resurrection life of love and joy and inner peace; we can start now. When Jesus broke through death and took his humanity into heaven, all kinds of possibilities were opened up for us.

The book of Job was written long before Jesus' time, and yet with amazing foreknowledge he talks of knowing his redeemer lives. Read Job 19:23-27a, and see how it looks forward to the person and work of Jesus.

Next look at the Sadducees and their trick question for Jesus. Use pictures of men and a woman cut from a mail-order catalogue to accompany the complicated situation, and stop before finding out what Jesus said for their own ideas of a reply. Then read what Jesus said, trying to tease out the way he replied to their fears and misunderstandings, rather than the question itself.

Obviously this is an area where some false teaching could easily creep into the Church, and sure enough it did. Read 2 Thessalonians 2:1-5, 13-17 and work out what these false rumours had been saying. Paul is determined about us standing firm and sticking to the teaching which goes directly back to when Jesus was walking about visibly in person.

Things to discuss

1. Why do you think many who would call themselves Christians find it difficult to accept the reality of life after death?

2. Pool any remembered references in the Bible that point to life after death being a reality, and look up some others using a concordance. Using these, how would you help someone to understand more about heaven?

Seeing and believing

Thought for the day — Having seen Jesus in person, the disciples are convinced of the Resurrection. We too can meet him personally.

Things to read — Acts 5:27-32
John 20:19-29

Things to do

Aim: To look at the importance we place on seeing in order to believe, and how Jesus honoured this for Thomas and the other apostles.

Use the following 'Convince them' exercise, where they have to try and persuade their partner that a tall story is true.

- You had completed your essay before the deadline but your dad accidentally threw it out for recycling!
- Your new-born baby cousin weighed in at 16 lbs!
- You saw your cat do a triple somersault and land on the tip of its tail!

Did they believe you?

Fill in the background to the Acts reading, and then read today's section together. As in our starter activity, Peter was trying to convince the Sanhedrin of something they didn't believe was true. But there was a big difference. The apostles were actually eye-witnesses of the risen Jesus, and so they knew they were speaking about something that had really happened.

Look at the account in John's Gospel of the events that took place on Easter Sunday evening, and the following week when Thomas was with them. Use the sheet to guide you in the discussion about it, so that they are able to draw out some of the factors involved in being convinced, and in recognising and perceiving things with or without the aid of visual evidence.

Things to discuss

1. How do you think the apostles felt when they found Jesus there among them for the first time since the last supper?

2. What would you say to someone who felt they could only believe in God if they could see him?

Index of Uses

TOPICS

Anger	10, 38
Argument	58
Baptism	23, 27, 76-7
Beatitudes	46-7, 60
Bible	84-5
Bones	26
Building	48-9
Bullying	57
Challenge	68
Change	63, 66, 70-1, 87
Childhood	19, 20
Choosing	74
Church	35, 60-1, 63, 64, 73, 76, 81
Clothing	20-1
Commitment	36, 78-9
Conflict	38, 58
Cost	36
Creation	8
Cross	39, 50, 80
Danger	18, 37
Death	26-7, 51, 88-9, 90
Discipleship	34-44
Disease	66
Disobedience	30
Doctor	70
Easter	90
Encouragement	72
Endurance	40-1
Enemies	56, 59
Envy	10
Example	60-1
Faith	42, 46, 90
Faithfulness	40, 42-3, 78-9
Fire	64
Forgiveness (God's)	9, 10, 66, 70, 72
Forgiveness (Ours)	58-9
Friend	39, 56
Fruit	55
Generosity (God's)	10, 14
Growth	20, 39, 66
Happiness	46
Healing	66, 68-9
Holy Spirit	62-3, 64, 76, 84
Improve	66, 68
Incarnation	20
Journey	18, 34-5, 38
King	24-5
Knowledge (God's)	50
Law	49, 54, 68-9, 74, 82-3, 84
Life	26
Life after death	26-7, 88-9, 90
Listen	86-7
Love	54-5, 56-7, 58, 78-9, 80-1
Marriage	78-9
Mercy (God's)	10
Messiah	22-3, 43, 68, 76
Mission	34
Need	12
New creation	66
Newspapers	80
Obedience	30, 42
Palm Sunday	24-5
Patience	40, 66
Pentecost	64
Persecution	61
Plumb line	74
Prayer	9, 12, 14, 42, 64, 69, 84-5
Presence (God's)	40
Priorities	46, 50
Provision (God's)	12-13, 14
Renewal	66
Repentance	70-1, 87
Rescue	18
Responsibility	72

Resurrection	26-7, 51, 88, 90
Revelation	11, 28-9, 83, 86
Riches	52-3
Rock	48
Sabbath	68
Safety	18
Saints	60-1
Save	9
Sin	30, 51, 71, 73
Storm	8
Strengthen	40
Suffering	25, 38-9, 40-1
Support	72
Temptation	30-1, 44, 51
Trust	42, 46, 63
Truth	68, 86
Understand	82
Wait	42, 64
Warning	72-3
Water	13, 76
Wedding	13, 78-9
Wine	13
Word	28-9, 86

Joseph (NT)	18
Joshua	40
Judas	24
Lazarus	24, 26
Martha	27
Mary (Mother of Jesus)	18, 24
Mary (Friend of Jesus)	27
McClung (Floyd)	40
Moses	11, 18
Naaman	66
Nehemiah	86
Nicodemus	62
Peter	24, 38, 66, 77, 90
Pharisee	14, 24
Paul	11, 21, 27, 30, 34, 40, 49, 51, 88
Samuel	20
Satan	44
Simeon	42-3
Tax collector	14
Ten Boom (Corrie)	59
Thomas	90
Timothy	40
Tutu (Desmond)	40

PEOPLE

Abraham	9
Adam	30-1
Amos	74
Anna	42-3
Elijah	13
Elisha	66
Eve	30
Ezekiel	26
Isaiah	14, 23
Jeremiah	38, 47
Jesus	18-31
Job	88
John the Baptist	23, 70
Jonah	10
Joseph (OT)	58

ACTIVITIES

Bible references	84, 89
Card game	68
Drama	24, 52, 58, 70, 78
Dressing up	20
Following instructions	22, 28, 73
Guessing game	74
Imagining	64
Maps	38
Memory game	52
Modelling clay	66
Music	21, 67, 88
Newspaper cuttings	80
Picture design	61
Picture focus	24, 26
Picture puzzle	11, 48, 82

Index of Uses

Quiz	82, 84, 88
Rearrange in order	46, 50, 60, 62
Rearrange in groups	56
Science	8
Searching	9, 18
Sharing ideas	10, 24, 64, 76, 80, 86
Story telling	90
Team games	12, 86
Tests of skill	14, 30, 34, 36, 40, 52, 54, 66, 72
Trust game	42
Word puzzle	50
Yes-No game	44

BIBLE REFERENCES

Genesis 1:1-3	28
Genesis 2:4b-9, 15-25	8
Genesis 2:15-17; 3:1-7	30
Genesis 18:20-32	9
Genesis 45:3-11, 15	58
Exodus 3:7-10	18
Exodus 19:2-8a	34
Exodus 23:4, 5, 9	56
Exodus 33:18-23	11
Leviticus 19:9-18	80
Leviticus 19:15-18	54
Deuteronomy 5:1-22	82
Deuteronomy 8:1-6	44
Deuteronomy 11:18-21, 26-28	48
Deuteronomy 30:15-20	74
Joshua 1:1-9	40
1 Samuel 3:1-10	20
1 Kings 17:8-16	12
2 Kings 5:1-14	66
Nehemiah 8:1-3, 5-12	86
Job 19:23-27a	88
Psalm 1	46, 54
Psalm 15	60
Psalm 19:7-11	86
Psalm 37:3-9	42
Psalm 65:6-13	8
Psalm 85	9
Psalm 103:1-13	10
Psalm 104:10-24	14
Psalm 119:97-106	84
Proverbs 3:1-12	36
Ecclesiastes 2:1-11	52
Isaiah 43:1-2	76
Isaiah 49:1-7	22
Isaiah 50:4-10	24
Isaiah 58:9b-12	14
Isaiah 62:1-5	78
Jeremiah 1:4-10	68
Jeremiah 7:1-7	68
Jeremiah 15:15-21	38
Jeremiah 17:5-10	46
Jeremiah 31:31-34	84
Ezekiel 33:7-11	72
Ezekiel 37:1-14	26, 62
Daniel 6:6-13, 16-23	50
Amos 7:7-17	74
Jonah 3:10-4:11	10
Habakkuk 2:1-4	42
Malachi 3:1-4	70
Matthew 2:13-23	18
Matthew 4:1-11	30
Matthew 5:1-12	60
Matthew 5:17-48	82
Matthew 5:38-48	56
Matthew 7:21-29	48
Matthew 9:35-10:10	34
Matthew 10:24-39	50
Matthew 16:21-25	38
Matthew 18:15-20	72
Matthew 20:1-16	10
Matthew 22:34-40	54
Luke 2:22-40	42
Luke 2:41-52	20
Luke 3:1-6	70
Luke 3:15-17, 21-22	76
Luke 4:16-30	86
Luke 6:17-26	46
Luke 6:27-38	58

Index of Uses

Luke 8:22-25	8	Romans 3:21-26	34
Luke 10:25-37	74	Romans 5:12-19	30
Luke 11:1-13	9	Romans 6:1-11	26, 50
Luke 12:13-21	52	Romans 7:18-8:4	48
Luke 12:35-43	40	Romans 12:3-18	72
Luke 13:10-17	68	Romans 12:14-21	56
Luke 14:25-33	36	Romans 13:8-10	82
Luke 18:1-8	84	1 Corinthians 10:12-13	44
Luke 18:9-14	14	2 Corinthians 4:1-6	11
Luke 19:28-40	24	2 Corinthians 9:6-12	12
Luke 20:27-38	88	Ephesians 1:1-6	60
John 1:1-18	28	Ephesians 4:1-3, 31-32	58
John 1:14-18	11	Ephesians 5:21-33	78
John 1:29-42	22	Philippians 2:5-8	20
John 2:1-11	12, 78	2 Thessalonians 2:1-5, 13-17	88
John 3:1-12	62	1 Timothy 6:6-19	52
John 11:1-45	26	2 Timothy 1:1-14	40
John 13:31-35	80	2 Timothy 3:14-4:5	84
John 14:8-17, 25-27	64	Hebrews 1:1-3	28
John 20:19-29	90	Hebrews 2:10-18	18, 38
John 21:15-19	66	Hebrews 10:19-31	68
Acts 2:1-4	62	Hebrews 12:3-11	36
Acts 2:1-21	64	James 1:16-27	66
Acts 5:27-32	90	1 Peter 2:9	60
Acts 8:14-17	76	1 John 4:7-12	80